The Best Ever
Baking Book

Jane Bull

A Dorling Kindersley Book

Design and text Jane Bull
Editor Violet Peto
Design Assistant Eleanor Bates
Photographer Andy Crawford
Producer, Pre-Production Nadine King
Producer Amy Knight
Jacket Designer Amy Keast
Jacket Coordinator Francesca Young
Managing Editor Penny Smith
Managing Art Editor Mabel Chan
Publisher Mary Ling

First published in Great Britain in 2017 by
Dorling Kindersley Limited
80 Strand, London, WC2R 0RL

Copyright © 2017 Dorling Kindersley Limited
A Penguin Random House Company
10 9 8 7 6 5 4 3 2 1
001–308183–Oct/2017

A CIP catalogue record for this book
is available from the British Library.
ISBN: 978-0-2413-1816-4

Material used in this book
was previously published in:
The Baking Book (2005)
The Cooking Book (2002)

Printed and bound in China

A WORLD OF IDEAS:
SEE ALL THERE IS TO KNOW

www.dk.com

Bring out the chunky cookies

Bake a batch of . . .

cherry pies or clever scones...

...then whisk up a mountain

Baking basics

Getting started

Here are the things you will need to bake the recipes in this book.

Weigh out your ingredients before you start, that way you won't leave anything out.

Warning! Look out for this sign and take care.

Safe baking

- When you see this sign ask an adult to help you.
- An adult should always be around when you are in the kitchen.
- Ovens are HOT – wear your oven gloves.

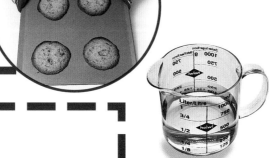

Weighing out

REMEMBER if you start a recipe using grams then stick to them. Don't mix up grams and ounces in one recipe.

MEASURING SPOONS – these are very useful. They have standard sizes from tablespoons to half teaspoons.

Measuring jug for measuring liquids.

Weighing scales for measuring dry ingredients.

Measuring spoons for measuring small amounts e.g salt.

Kitchen rules

BE PREPARED – Lay out all the ingredients and utensils that you will need for the recipe.

CLEAN UP – always wash your hands before you cook.

COVER UP – Wear an apron to protect your clothes.

WASH & TIDY UP – It's your mess, you clear it up. Keep the kitchen tidy as you go along. Then you can cook again!

How long will it take?

The clock symbol gives you helpful information on timings such as how long to bake the recipe, knead dough, or leave it to rise.

How much will it make?

This symbol tells you how much the recipe will make e.g 12 cookies or 24 mini breads.

Your baking kit

WOODEN SPOON

COOKIE CUTTERS

SPOONS

FORK

KNIFE

PASTRY BRUSH

BAKING SHEET

ROLLING PIN

LOAF TIN

LOTS OF BOWLS

ELECTRIC WHISK

MUFFIN TIN

MIXING BOWL

BUN TIN

YOUR (CLEAN) HANDS

COOLING RACK

GREASEPROOF PAPER

CAKE TINS 18 CM (7 IN)

Cookie collection

To start you off

all you need are three things:

Plain flour + **Caster sugar** + **Butter** = ☺ **24 cookies**

150g (6 oz)   50g (2 oz)   100g (4 oz)   plain shortbread

Mmmm They look good!

1 recipe x 10

These aren't just ordinary cookies – with a little pinch here and a spot of decoration there, you can make 10 completely different cookies. 10 cookies in one!

1

2

3

4

5

6

7

8

9

10

yum yum

Turn the page
to discover the
magic ingredients.

7

How to make shortbread cookies

Rubbing in – This is the way you mix the flour, butter, and sugar together. Rub the mixture between your thumb and fingertips until it looks like breadcrumbs (see page 60).

COOKIE EQUIPMENT

MIXING BOWL BAKING TRAY FORK COOLING RACK

1 In it all goes

Put all the ingredients into the bowl!

Flour Sugar Butter

2 Rub it together

Rub the mixture between your thumbs and fingertips. Add flavours now

3 Make a ball

When the mixture looks crumbly, squeeze it together to make a ball of dough.

4 Roll little balls

Pinch off little lumps of dough, and roll them to the size of a ping-pong ball.

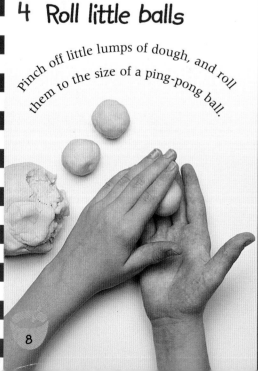

5 Squash them

Place the balls on a baking sheet, leaving room for them to spread when they cook.

Press flat with a fork

Or try using your thumb instead to press them down.

6 Bake them

Set the oven 170°C/325°F/Gas mark 3. Bake for 15-20 mins, cool on a rack.

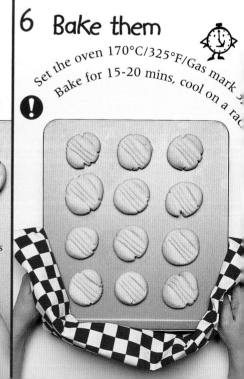

8

1 Chocolate chips
50g (2oz)

2 Cocoa powder
25g (1oz)

3 Coconut
50g (2oz)

4 Cinnamon
1 teaspoon

5 Sweeties
Press these into the cookies
before you bake them.

Peanuts

6 Peanut butter
1 tablespoon

7 Raisins
50g (2oz)

8 Almond essence
Add a few drops of almond essence
and stick an almond on the top.

9 Sugar strands
25g (1oz)

10 Chopped nuts
50g (2oz)

How to make 10 new cookies

**Add your flavours at
step 2.** If you want flavoured
cookies, then add your cocoa,
chocolate chips, coconut, or
cinnamon at stage 2 when your
mixture is crumbly. Decorate your
cookies with the nuts or sweets
just before you bake them.

Now get creative
with your cookie
cutters, see over
the page.

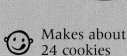
Bake me!

Create and bake

Make more of your cookie dough –
roll it out, cut out some shapes, then have
fun with icing.

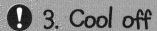
Cookie dough
See page 8.

Makes about
24 cookies

1. Roll out the dough

Sprinkle flour on your work surface and
a rolling pin. Now roll out
your dough until
it's 5mm (¼ in)
thick, then choose
your cookie
cutters and get
shaping!

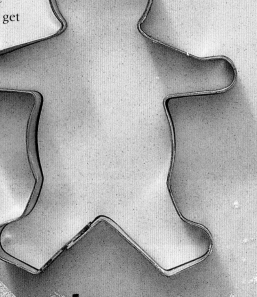

2. Ready to bake

Grease a baking tray (see page 61)
and place your shapes on
it, leaving spaces
between them.

Bake for
15 minutes.

Preheat the oven to
170°C/325°F/
Gas mark 3.

3. Cool off

Carefully remove the tray from
the oven. Let the cookies cool
a little on the tray, then transfer
to a cooling rack.

Tip – If it is difficult to roll, cut
the ball of dough in half, and roll out
one half at a time.

Ice and sprinkle

Icing –
Mix up some icing sugar and water with drops of food colouring.

Icing sugar
3 tablespoons

Water
3 teaspoons

Food colouring

Now add some sprinkles.

Icing mix

Put 3 tablespoons of icing sugar in a bowl, add 3 teaspoons of water, and stir it in. Add more water if the icing is too thick.

Spoon the icing over the cookies and decorate them.

Adding colour

Use a cocktail stick to add colour to the icing mix. Keep adding and stirring until it's the colour you want.

A fun-filled box of cookies

Make holes with the end of a straw. Do this before you bake the cookie.

Use a cocktail stick to make smaller features like eyes.

Cut out a shape, then use a smaller cutter to make a new shape.

Chocolate chunk cookies

Forget shop-bought

cookies, these are much tastier!
Use a good quality chocolate
chopped up into big chunks.

Makes 12 cookies

EQUIPMENT

MIXING BOWL

SPOON

KNIFE

WOODEN SPOON

BAKING TRAY

PASTRY BRUSH

COOLING RACK

Butter

Sugar (brown and caster)

Soft butter is easier to mix with the sugar.

1 Start creaming

See page 62 to beat an egg.

Preheat the oven to 190°C/375°F/Gas mark 5.

2 Add beaten egg

Mix in the flour.

3 Stir in the flour

Get help to chop the chunks.

4 Add choc chunks

Spoon four heaps on each tray.

5 Spoon onto tray

Bake for 10–12 minutes then take out of the oven and cool on a rack.

6 Bake them

Prepare the tray for the next batch of cookies.

Let them cool before moving to a rack.

7 Cooling down

Eat them when they are still warm

Choc tip

Stick chunks of chocolate on top of the heaps before cooking.

Flour	Butter	Water	Red jam
175g (6oz) plain flour	90g (3oz)	About 6 tsp	125g (4oz)

Gem tarts and cheesy flans

Sweet or savoury – these tarts can be both. A jammy teatime treat or a cheesy mini-meal. Pop them into your lunchbox as delicious snacks.

Shortcrust pastry

Once you know how to make this pastry, you'll find that you can make lots of dishes. You can make apple pies, mince pies, sausage rolls, bigger flans and quiches, and much more.

= 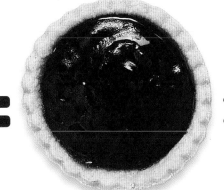 ×

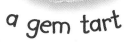
a gem tart

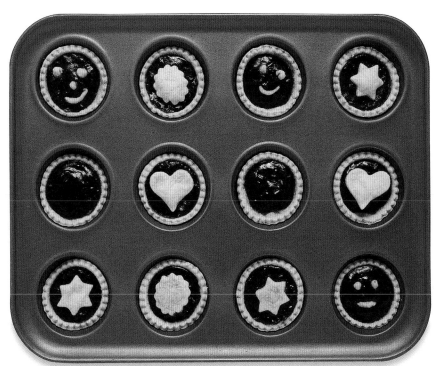

Roll out the gem tarts

When you make the **shortcrust pastry** it is essential that you don't put in too much water, add a little at a time. Succeed with your tarts and you can call yourself a professional pastry chef! Experiment with fillings and test them on your family.

GEM TART TOOLS

LARGE MIXING BOWL   COOLING RACK   BUN TIN

SPOON   7.5 CM (3 IN) PASTRY CUTTER   ROLLING-PIN

Try these savoury cheese tarts

Collect up:

Shortcrust pastry (same as the gem tarts)
2 eggs
60g (2oz) grated cheese
150ml (¼ pint) milk

1. Prepare the pastry in the same way as for the gem tarts.
2. Beat up the eggs in a bowl. Add the grated cheese and milk.
3. Spoon the mixture into the pastry cases.
4. Bake them in the same way as the gem tarts.

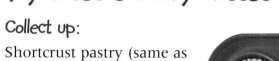

Top them off with half a Cherry tomato

1 Rub together
the flour and butter with your fingers

5 Make a ball of pastry
The bowl will be clean when it's ready

9 Cut the cases
The bits left over can be shaped and cooked

2 Keep rubbing

until the mixture looks like breadcrumbs.

3 Add some water

Add six teaspoons to the mixture.

4 Squeeze it

Bring the mixture together into a ball.

6 Sprinkle flour

over the ball, rolling pin, and the table.

! Set the oven to 200°C/400°F/Gas mark 6.

Turn the pastry as you roll it. Add flour to the table if it sticks.

7 Press down the ball

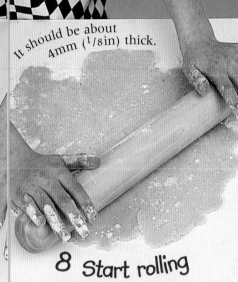

It should be about 4mm (1/8in) thick.

8 Start rolling

10 Spoon in the filling

Only half fill the cases with jam.

11 Bake the tarts

Bake in the oven for about 15 minutes. **!**

Royal tarts for the queen of hearts

Leave them to cool – if you can wait!

Cherry pies

Fill buttery pastry pies

with sweet fillings and feed them
to your sweetheart.

Tinned
cherry pie
filling

Pastry
From pages 16-19

+

Pie filling
200g (8oz) can

=

× 12 pies

Fruity pie fillings

When it's late summer, get out
and pick your own fresh
fruit. Soft fruits, such as
blackberries, are perfect
and mix well with apple.
Alternatively you can
buy canned pie filling
or try some of these
other yummy ideas.

☺

Makes
12 pies

Serve up your pies with a dusting of icing sugar and spoonful of custard

Unlike tarts, pies have lids. Make your lids by cutting shapes from extra pastry.

All kinds of pies

Apple pie

Peel and chop some eating apples and put them into a saucepan with a little sugar and a couple of tablespoons of water. Boil them until they are soft and when the mixture is cool, spoon it into pastry cases.

Mince pie

Just right for Christmas – a jar of mince meat is packed full of sultanas, peel, and raisins. Simply pop it in the pastry case.

Lemon curd pie

For a tangy taste, buy a jar of lemon curd. Spoon it straight into the cases and pop on the lid.

Red berry jam pie

Sweet strawberry or raspberry jam makes a perfect partner for the plain pastry case.

Marmalade pie

For a rich, zesty taste try using orange marmalade with thick peel.

Moon rocks

Your mission – to reconstruct moon rocks that are good enough to eat. Read the scientific data carefully and report back at teatime.

This is what moon rocks are made of:

One pinch of salt.

| 250g (8oz) self-raising flour | 90g (3oz) soft brown sugar | 90g (3oz) butter | 125g (4oz) raisins | 1/2 teaspoon mixed spice | 1 egg |

Collect these samples together, then turn the page to receive your instructions for moon rock construction.

 Makes 8-12 moon rocks

One small step for man, one giant heap of cake for me!

Other space rocks to find

Leave out the raisins and try out these other tasty rocks.

Comet cocktail

125 g (4 oz) chocolate chips

Meteor shower

125 g (4 oz) sugar strands

Mars attack

Add 1 tsp of red food colouring at the same time as the egg.

Mission moon rock

Collect up your samples and prepare your work area. Check the tools and follow these instructions to proceed. Remember captain, you must be back from a successful mission in time for tea. GOOD LUCK.

MISSION EQUIPMENT

MIXING BOWL

FORK

BAKING TRAY

COOLING RACK

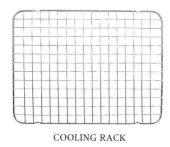

1 Throw in the butter and flour

Rub it between your fingers and thumbs until it looks like breadcrumbs.

2 Add the sugar and raisins

Mix them up evenly using your hands. Add the mixed spice as well.

6 Grease the tray

Spread some butter over the tray.

 Set the oven to 200°C/400°F/Gas mark 6.

7 Form rocky heaps

Make about 8-12 heaps, keeping them quite rough. Then put them in the ove

3 Beat the egg in a separate bowl

Then add the beaten egg to the mixture.

4 Mix it together with a fork

Make sure it is all mixed up properly.

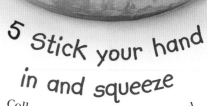

5 Stick your hand in and squeeze

Collect up all the bits in the bowl and squeeze them together into a ball.

Yummy! A successful mission, captain!

Leave them to cool on a rack.

8 Bake them

Bake in the oven for about 15 minutes.

Tweetie pies

Crunchy nuts and seeds aren't just for birds – they make tasty nibbles to snack on anytime, even breakfast!

Tweetie Pies

You will need:

Butter.
150g (6oz)

Soft brown sugar
100g (4oz)

Porridge oats
225g (8oz)

Honey
2 tablespoons

Now go nuts!

Add one of these **or** why not add them all?

Sultanas

Sesame seeds

Peanuts

Try 2 tablespoons
of each nut, seed, or fruit

Pumpkin
seeds

Sunflower
seeds

Pine nuts

Coconut

Chopped
nuts

 Makes 18 pies

Mix up some pies

Crunchy pies – The longer you bake them, the crunchier they will get, and each bite will contain a completely different crunch!

 Preheat the oven to 190°C/375°F/ Gas mark 5.

TWEETY PIE TOOLS

MIXING BOWL

WOODEN SPOON

KNIFE

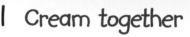
DESSERT SPOON

PASTRY BRUSH

BUN TIN

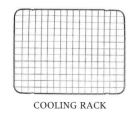
COOLING RACK

28

Mix the butter and sugar together with a wooden spoon until the mixture is creamy.

1 Cream together

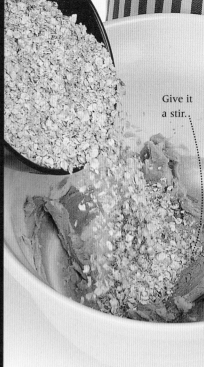

Give it a stir.

2 Tip in the oats

Spoon up some mixture and roll it in a ball.

5 Make the pies

Grease the tin, then put in the ball of mixture.

6 Press them down

Then give
it another
stir.

Add as many as
you like and stir
them in.

3 Pour in the honey

4 Go nuts!

Bake in the oven for
10 to 15 minutes.

7 Into the oven !

Use a knife to lift
them out of the tray.

They will keep
in an airtight tin
for two to three
weeks.

8 Leave to cool

Come for tea!

Fruit
Any dried fruit can be used. These are raisin scones spread with butter.

Sweet
Try these sweet scones with jam and cream.

Cheesy
These savoury scones are topped with grated cheese for an even tastier treat.

It's teatime!

Scones for tea – invite your friends round for sweet and savoury treats.

Butter
50g (2oz)

+

Self-raising flour
225g (8oz)

+

Milk
120ml (4fl oz)

=

1 plain scone

Makes 8 slices

Clever scones

Use this plain scone mixture to create new recipes. Just add all sorts of ingredients from sugar, dried fruit, and seeds to olives and cheese. Make a meal of them!

More tea, Owl? Have a scone with it.

Add the sugar OR fruit OR cheese at this stage.

Rub the butter and flour together to make breadcrumbs.

Mix the flavour in.

1 Rub together

2 Add the flavours

3 Pour in the milk

Scones x 3

Make sweet or savoury – Follow the steps the same way for all the recipes. But at step 2 choose the flavour you want and mix it in. Then bake and enjoy them fresh from the oven.

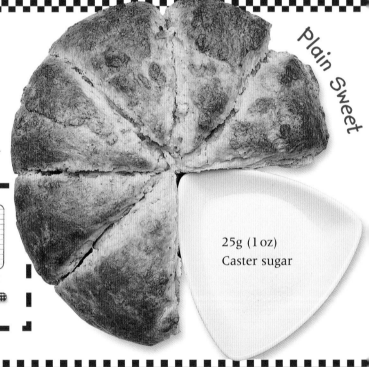

Plain Sweet

25g (1 oz) Caster sugar

EQUIPMENT

BAKING TRAY

COOLING RACK

MIXING BOWL

PASTRY BRUSH   KNIFE

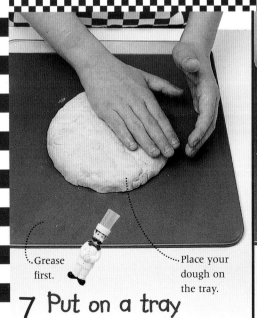

..Grease first.

..Place your dough on the tray.

7 Put on a tray

..Divide the dough up – 8 pieces works best.

8 Cut into sections

..Brush with milk for a glossy finish.

9 Get ready to bake

Use a knife to stir the mixture.

4 Stir with a knife

Bring all the mixture together.

5 Make a ball

Flour a clean surface.

Flatten the ball to about 3cm (1 in) thick.

Don't handle the dough too much.

6 Flour and flatten

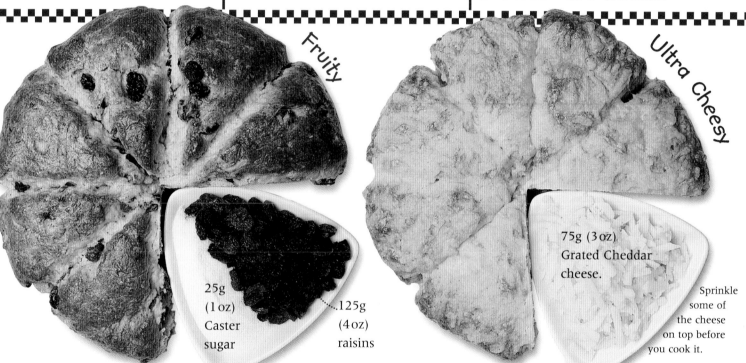

Fruity

25g (1 oz) Caster sugar

125g (4 oz) raisins

Ultra Cheesy

75g (3 oz) Grated Cheddar cheese.

Sprinkle some of the cheese on top before you cook it.

❗ Preheat the oven to 220°C/425°/ Gas mark 7.

Bake for 25 minutes, take out of the oven, and cool on a rack.

Scone tip

Eat it on the same day as you bake it.

I like to eat it fresh from the oven.

10 All done

Rainbow cakes

Heaps of colourful rainbow cakes cover the party table. Bake little cakes and decorate them however you like. Add your own fairy cake magic!

Magic up some fairy cakes

A measure, a whisk, or the swish of a wand.

125g (4oz)
self-raising flour

125g (4oz)
butter (room temperature)

125g (4oz)
caster sugar

1 tsp baking powder

2 eggs

1 tsp vanilla essence

Makes 24 little cakes

LITTLE CAKE UTENSILS

MIXING BOWL

TEASPOON

TABLESPOON

SIEVE

COOLING RACK

ELECTRIC WHISK

Fill them with paper cake cases

2 BUN TINS

Rainbow icing

Mix up lots of little bowls of different coloured icing. For green icing, mix yellow and blue; for orange, mix yellow and red. Use anything sweet to decorate the tops, such as glacé cherries, raisins, sweets, etc.

To ice 4 cakes:

1 tbsp icing sugar
1 tsp water
1 drop food colouring

1. Stir together the water, food colouring, and icing sugar.

2. Drop a small dollop of icing into the centre of the cake and let it spread.

3. Decorate it with anything sweet, and use tubes of writing icing for extra patterns.

Sieving adds more air.

1 Sieve the flour and baking powder

Set the oven to 190ºC/375ºF/Gas mark

5 Fill up the cases

Put a teaspoon of mixture in each case

Bake in the oven for 20 minutes.

3 Whisk until it's creamy

4 Does it drop off a spoon?

If it drops off easily in a dollop, then it's ready.

2 Add everything else

Beat the eggs and throw them in with the butter, sugar, and vanilla essence.

6 Take out of the oven

❗

Shhh... Cakes cooling

Meringue mountain

Egg whites
2 whites

+

Caster sugar
125g (4oz)

=

Makes about
12 small peaks

See page 62 for how
to separate an egg.

Fruity nest

Spoon thick cream onto a nest and top it off with pieces of fruit.

Peak sandwich

Sandwich two meringue peaks together with thick cream.

Mmmmeringue

Meringues are made from egg whites mixed with sugar baked in a very cool oven until they are crunchy on the outside and soft inside – mmmm!

Serve up your meringues with cream and fruit or just on their own.

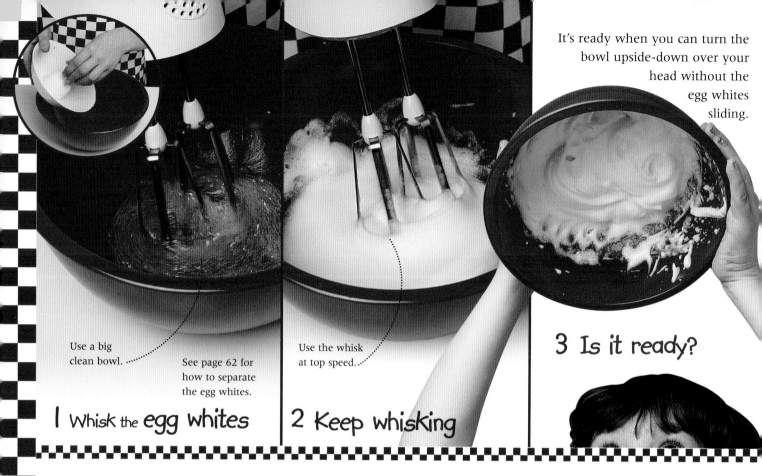

It's ready when you can turn the bowl upside-down over your head without the egg whites sliding.

Use a big clean bowl.

See page 62 for how to separate the egg whites.

Use the whisk at top speed.

3 Is it ready?

1 Whisk the egg whites

2 Keep whisking

Whisk up a mountain

Whisking is fun – An electric whisk makes the egg white froth up quicker than by hand, but remember to stop it spinning before you take it out of the bowl, or you'll cover the kitchen!

Meringue hints and tips

• Whisk the egg whites just enough – try the "over the head" test as in step 3.
• Add the sugar a tablespoon at a time while whisking. Keep repeating this until all the sugar is used up.
• Grease the tray first to stop the paper slipping.

Grease the tray then cover with greaseproof paper.

Preheat the oven to 140°C/275°F/Gas mark 1.

7 Spoon out some peaks

Pour in the sugar – about a tablespoon at a time.

4 Add some sugar and whisk

Whisk in the sugar BUT not at full speed.

5 Keep whisking

See page 61 for whisking tips.

When all the sugar is in, give the mixture a final whisk.

The mixture should look glossy and stand up in peaks.

6 Now it's peaky

EQUIPMENT

MIXING BOWL

ELECTRIC WHISK

TEASPOON AND DESSERT SPOON

GREASEPROOF PAPER

BAKING SHEET

PASTRY BRUSH

Press the peak down with a spoon to make a nest.

Make a snowman with peaks joined together.

(!) 🕐 Bake in the oven for 2 hours.

8 Ready to bake

(!) Take the meringues out of the oven.

Leave them for a few hours to dry out.

9 All dried out

Happy birthday Bear!
Let's have a party,
we can ask Owl to come.

Yes please!

42

Bake a cake

...and celebrate with this chocolate-covered treat. Share it with your special friends when you have a reason to say...
"Let's have a party!"

Mmm chocolate

Makes 8–12 slices

How's your cake Little Ted?

All-in-one mix

Simply beat all the ingredients together in the bowl.

This recipe makes a plain sponge cake. Baking two cakes means you can layer them up and fill the middle with jam or fresh cream. You can also add flavour to the mixture like cocoa powder, dried fruit, or vanilla.

Flour
125g (4oz)
Self-raising flour

Eggs
2 large

Butter
125g (4oz)
Softened butter

Sugar
125g (4oz)
Caster sugar

Baking powder
1 teaspoon

Bake a cake

Sponge cake

Divide the mixture evenly between two lined tins (see page 61). Spread the mixture flat so the cake rises evenly. Let them cool down before you spread on the topping. Keep the cake in a cool place and eat within two days.

Preheat the oven to 170°C/325°F/ Gas mark 3 **!**

Top and fill

Chocolate cream

Use good quality chocolate mixed with double cream. Melt the chocolate first then spoon in the cream.

Chocolate
200g (7oz)

Whipped cream
6 tablespoons

Prepare the tins (see page 61)........

.... Share the mixture between the tins.

1 Fill the tins

Spread the mixture out to the sides evenly.

Bake in the oven for 20 minutes **!**

2 Spread the mixture

Stir the chunks around to help them melt.

Take care, HOT water. **!**

1 Melt the chocolate

Take the bowl away from the hot water.

.... Stir the cream into the melted chocolate.

2 Add the cream

Make the mixture

Put all the ingredients into a bowl and whisk together for two minutes. Keep the whisk on a low setting.

EQUIPMENT

MIXING BOWL

ELECTRIC WHISK

KNIFE

SPOON

WIRE RACK

2 CAKE TINS 18 CM (7 IN)

PASTRY BRUSH

GREASEPROOF PAPER

Melting choc

To melt the chocolate, pour very hot water into a bowl. Sit another bowl on top and pop the chocolate in. The heat from the water will melt it.

Break the chocolate into chunks first.

Take care – HOT water.

Very hot water – don't over fill the bowl.

Run a knife around the edge where the cake may stick to the tin.

Allow the cakes to cool down.

3 Out of the oven

Hold the rim of the tin.

Give it a bit of a tap.

Tip the cake out of the tin.

4 Remove the cakes

Carefully peel back the paper.

The cakes should be cold before adding the topping.

5 Leave to get cold

Place the top layer on

Put two spoonfuls on the bottom layer.

Spread it over with a knife.

3 Spread the filling

Spoon on the rest of the mixture.

4 Pour on the topping

Use a knife to spread the mixture over the top and down the sides.

5 Spread it all over

Upside-down

Looks like a cake, but turn it over and it's a fruity pudding!

1 tsp baking powder

125g (4oz) self-raising flour

125g (4oz) butter

125g (4oz) caster sugar

2 eggs (beaten)

1 tsp vanilla essence

Hidden fruits to try: raisins, glacé cherries, tinned mandarin oranges, peaches, pineapple, apricots, or angelica

pudding

Serve up your pudding hot and steaming with ice cream

Makes one big pudding or 24 small ones

Turn a pudding upside-down!

All you do is make the cake back to front – start with the top and end with the bottom! For mini upside-down puddings, use a bun tin with individual portions. Have fun doing it the wrong way around!

Sieve the flour.

1 Put all of the cake ingredients in a bowl

UPSIDE-DOWN TOOLS

ELECTRIC WHISK

LARGE MIXING BOWL

SIEVE

20 CM (8 IN) DIAMETER CAKE TIN WITH LOOSE BASE

LARGE SPOON

KNIFE

SERVING PLATE

BUN TIN FOR MINI PUDDINGS

4 Arrange the fruit
Lay the fruit face down so the pudding looks better at the end.

8 Cover with a plate

9 Now flip it over
Using oven gloves, put one hand on each side.

It's ready when it falls easily off the spoon in a dollop.

2 Whisk it until it's creamy

3 Grease the tin

❗ Set the oven to 190°C/375°F/Gas mark 5.

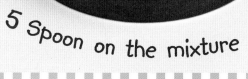

5 Spoon on the mixture

6 Smooth it out

❗ Put it in the oven.

7 Bake it ❗

🕐 Bake for 20 minutes.

10 Slide off the tin

Careful, it's hot! ❗

Monkey bread

Bakes like a cake
and slices like bread.
Monkey enjoys a piece
for tea or a snack in his
lunch box.

You'll go bananas over my yummy recipe!

You will need . . .

Butter
100g (4oz)

Self-raising flour
225g (8oz)

Soft brown sugar
100g (4oz)

Raisins
150g (6oz)

2 eggs

Honey
2 tablespoons

3 bananas

Butter
Flour

Rub the butter and flour together until they are like breadcrumbs.

1 Rubbing in

Add in sugar and raisins and give it a stir.

2 Add sugar and raisins

Beat the eggs, spoon out the honey, and stir them in.

3 Add eggs and honey

In a small bowl mash the bananas with a fork.

4 Mashed bananas

5 Add the bananas

6 Give it a stir

Dip the brush in oil and brush over the tin.

7 Grease the tin

Preheat the oven to 180°C/350°F/Gas mark 4.
Bake for 1 hour.

8 Pour it in

Is it cooked? Turn to page 61 to find out how to test it.

9 Leave to cool

Turn out your bread

Slide the knife between the cake and the tin.

10 Slide round a knife

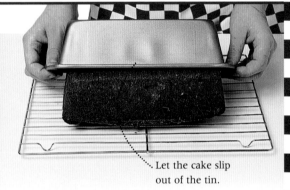

Let the cake slip out of the tin.

11 Flip over the tin

The cake will cut more easily when it's cold.

12 Nearly ready to eat!

Slice up the bread and serve it up

I like mine spread with butter

Mini monkey muffins

To make these yummy muffins, use the same mixture as the monkey bread but fill a muffin tin instead.

Makes 12 mini breads

MUFFIN TIN
AND
PAPER CASES

Just use your monkey bread mixture

Try these bread variations
instead of bananas...
apple and cinnamon

2 apples peeled and chopped

125ml (5 fl oz) milk

1 teaspoon cinnamon

Bunny bites

Grated peel and juice of an orange

2 carrots peeled and grated

1 teaspoon mixed spice

As in step 5 on the previous page.

Preheat the oven to 180°C/350°F/Gas mark 4.

1 Stir it up

Carefully spoon in the mixture.

2 Fill up the cases

Bake them for 15 minutes.

3 Bake your breads

Making variations

To make the variations, go back to step 5 of monkey bread, then instead of adding the banana put in the ingredients for apple or carrot breads and mix it all up in the same way.

Storage

Eat them warm or keep them fresh in an airtight tin. They'll keep for about two weeks.

Carrot bunny bites

Apple and cinnamon

Mini monkey muffins

Bits-in bread

Make bread taste more interesting by using grainy flour and sprinkles of seeds inside and out.

Bits-in bread is fun to bake and eat.

You will need:

Butter
25g (1oz)

Bits-in flour
225g (8oz)
Strong granary
bread flour

White flour
225g (8oz)
Strong white
bread flour

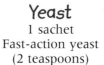

Yeast
1 sachet
Fast-action yeast
(2 teaspoons)

Sugar and salt
1 teaspoon
Brown sugar,
1 teaspoon Salt

Water
275ml (10fl oz)
Warm water

And a beaten egg
for a glossy
finish

Makes 12
rolls

Bits-in and on bread. As well as adding some seeds to your bread mixture, sprinkle a few on top – not just for decoration but because they make the bread taste good too!

You will need lots of different seeds

Sesame
seeds

Poppy
seeds

Sunflower
seeds

Pumpkin
seeds

55

Make a dip to pour the water in.

Mix it with a wooden spoon.

Put the flour, yeast, sugar, and salt in a bowl and rub in the butter.

Add some seeds now if you want more bits.

Make it a ball with your hands.

1 Rub together

2 Add water

3 Mix it up

How to make bread

Bread flour – It's important to use special bread flour, called strong flour. It comes in white, wholemeal, and granary, and for this recipe it has malt grains in it too.

Bread tips

Yeast likes warmth to help it grow and this will help your bread to rise.

• If all the things you work with are warm, such as the bowl and the room, this will help.

• Make sure the water isn't too hot or this will kill the yeast and your bread won't rise.

Grease the tray.

Place the dough balls on the tray.

Cover with clingfilm and leave in a warm place for about 40 minutes.

7 Prepare the tray

A beaten egg

When they have doubled in size, they are ready to decorate.

Brush them with beaten egg.

8 The rolls have grown!

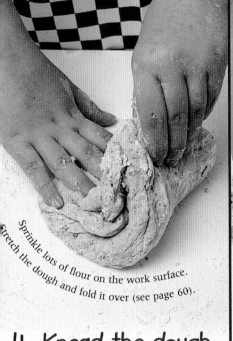
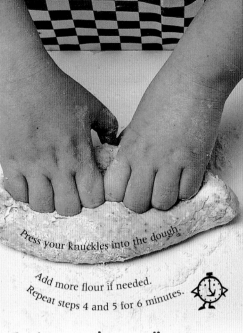

Sprinkle lots of flour on the work surface. Stretch the dough and fold it over (see page 60).

Press your knuckles into the dough. Add more flour if needed. Repeat steps 4 and 5 for 6 minutes.

Make into a ball and cut it into 12 even-sized pieces. Roll them into small balls.

4 Knead the dough | 5 Keep kneading | 6 Divide it up

Preheat the oven to 220°C/425°F/ Gas mark 7.

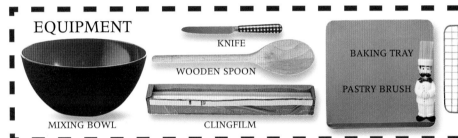

EQUIPMENT

KNIFE

WOODEN SPOON

MIXING BOWL

CLINGFILM

BAKING TRAY

PASTRY BRUSH

COOLING RACK

Now sprinkle on the seeds.

Serve up your rolls fresh from the oven with your favourite filling

Bake for 20 to 25 minutes, then take out of the oven and cool on a rack.

9 Get ready to bake

Mould your dough

Now it's time to play with your dough. Make a dough ball as shown before, but before you bake it try moulding it into different shapes.

Plaited bread

1 Roll your dough into three sausage shapes.

Cooking the shapes

Follow the steps as for bits-in bread, place your shapes on a greased tin, cover them, and allow them to rise until they are twice the size. Then bake for 25 minutes.

Dough balls

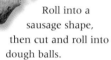

Roll into a sausage shape, then cut and roll into dough balls.

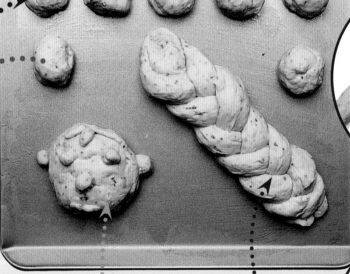

or a Pizza

Flatten a dough ball.

2 Squeeze your dough together at one end.

3 Bring one sausage over to the middle.

Grated cheese

Chopped olives

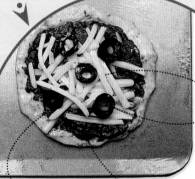

Spread a tablespoon of tomato purée on first.

Then a tablespoon of chopped tinned tomato.

2 Add some toppings, then bake in the oven.

Dough boy

Make small balls of dough and stick them to your rolls to make faces.

Repeat on the other side.

Carry on plaiting then squash the ends together and place on the tray.

Bake all kinds of bits-in fun

Bread tastes best when it's warm from the oven.

Try serving dough balls with garlic butter.

Garlic butter

59

You can bake

Baking Methods

Baking recipes use different methods to mix the same ingredients to achieve different results. Whether it's biscuits, cakes, or pastry, this book uses a few of the basic methods. Here they are with explanations of what they do.

Rubbing in

Using your thumb and fingertips, rub the butter and flour together until the mixture looks like breadcrumbs. This is used for a lot of the recipes in this book such as pastry and cookies.

Creaming

This is when you mix or beat the butter and sugar together with a wooden spoon so that they make a creamy mixture. In this book it's used for recipes like the chocolate chunk cookies.

Dough

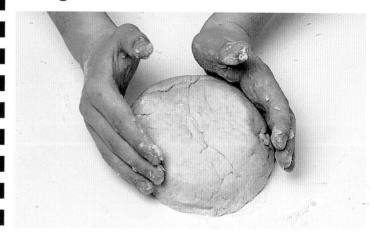

Dough is a name given to the mixture that makes pastry, biscuits, scones, or bread, but they behave differently when they are cooked. Bread dough needs kneading as this has yeast in it. Other dough should be handled lightly.

Tips

Let your dough rest in the fridge for half an hour before using it.

To store your dough wrap it in plastic and put in the fridge.

Cookie and pastry dough

Kneading

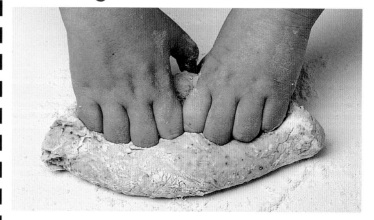

This is what you do to bread dough to get the yeast working. Fold the dough over itself and press your knuckles into it. Repeat this over and over again. Then leave it in a warm place to rise.

Whisking

Whisking egg whites can be done with a hand whisk but an electric one is much faster. Don't let any egg yolk in or it won't work. Whisk at full speed until the mixture stands up in peaks.

Is it cooked?

To check if the monkey bread is cooked, put a skewer in the centre of it when it's due to come out of the oven. If the skewer comes out with some mixture on it, it's not cooked so put it back in the oven.

To keep your cookies, cakes, and tweety pies fresh, store them in an AIRTIGHT tin and they will keep for a week or two.

Greasing baking tins

This will help to stop your bakes from sticking as they cook.

Put a little oil onto a pastry brush and sweep it all over the tin.

Oil

Line a tin with paper

To make sure your bakes have no chance of sticking, line the tin with greaseproof paper. Brush the tin with oil first so that the paper sticks to it.

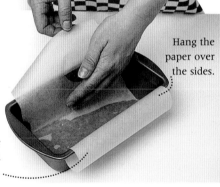

Hang the paper over the sides.

Use the paper to pull the cake out of the tin when the cake is cooked.

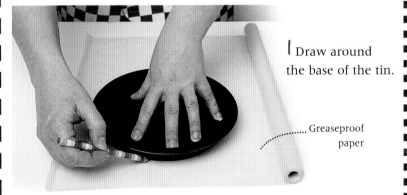

1 Draw around the base of the tin.

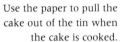

Greaseproof paper

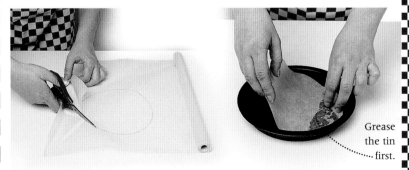

2 Cut out the shape.

3 Place the paper in the tin.

Grease the tin first.

Crack open an egg

How to get an egg out of the shell.

The secret is to be firm and gentle at the same time.

1 Tap the egg firmly against the edge of a bowl.

tap tap

2 Gently press your thumbs into the crack.

3 Pull the two shells apart and let the egg fall out.

White

Yellow yolk

Beating an egg

Mixing the egg white and yolk together.

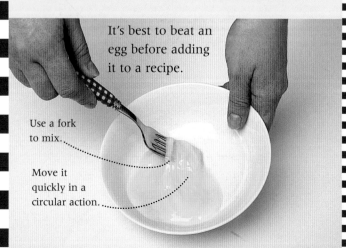

It's best to beat an egg before adding it to a recipe.

Use a fork to mix.

Move it quickly in a circular action.

Separate an egg – the easy way

Sometimes you will only want the egg white or the yolk. So you need to separate them carefully. It takes a bit of practice so have some spare eggs in case you break the yolk.

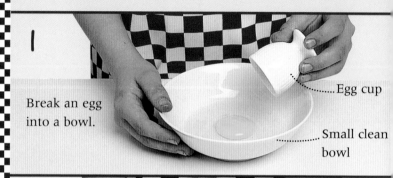

1 Break an egg into a bowl.

Egg cup

Small clean bowl

2 Cover the yolk with an egg cup.

Push the egg cup down.

3 Hold the egg cup down very firmly and tip the bowl.

Let the white fall into another bowl.

Meringue tip

Don't get any egg yolk in the egg white or your meringues won't work.

Put the yolk in another bowl.

Index

Acknowledgements

DK would like to thank: Charlotte, Billy, and James Bull, Seriya Ezigwe, Daniel Ceccarelli, Harry Holmstoel, Maisie Armah, and Jackelyn Hansard for modelling; Penelope Arlon, Sadie Thomas, and Laura Roberts for their work on the original content.
All images © Dorling Kindersley.
For further information see: www.dkimages.com